# By Gavin Edwards

*Illustrated by Chris Kalb*

**A Fireside Book** • Published by Simon & Schuster
New York  London  Toronto  Sydney  Tokyo  Singapore

# 'Scuse Me While I Kiss This Guy

## And Other Misheard Lyrics

FIRESIDE
Rockefeller Center
1230 Avenue of the Americas
New York, New York 10020

FIRESIDE and colophon are registered trademarks
of Simon & Schuster Inc.

Designed by Bonni Leon

Manufactured in the United States of America

13   15   17   19   20   18   16   14

Library of Congress Cataloging-in-Publication Data is available.

ISBN 0-671-50128-3

This book is dedicated to my parents,
who never took me to the doctor to
get my hearing checked.

# Introduction

My first misheard lyric came at the advanced age of six, when I learned to sing "Row, Row, Row Your Boat." I was convinced that the line after "merrily merrily merrily" was "life's a butter dream," rather than the more canonical "life is but a dream." I wasn't sure what visions of dairy products had to do with a boat trip, but I didn't have the courage to ask anybody.

Eventually my mistake was discovered in an elementary school chorus class, and I suffered the humiliation that can only be experienced in elementary school chorus classes. Although the shame eventually subsided, the pattern repeated itself for the rest of my life. Usually, it wasn't even a question of mulling over the lyrics and then getting them wrong. I would dive straight into a state of ignorance, and only be rudely corrected if I read a lyric sheet or heard somebody else singing the accurate version of a song.

The technical term for misheard lyrics is "mondegreens," coined by Sylvia Wright in a 1954 *Atlantic* article. As a child, young Sylvia had listened to a folk song that included the lines "They had slain the Earl of Moray/And Lady Mondegreen."

As is customary with the victims of misheard lyrics, she didn't realize her mistake for years. The song was not about the tragic fate of Lady Mondegreen, but rather, the continuing plight of the good earl: "They had slain the Earl of Moray/And laid him on the green."

Mondegreens can be found in every area of the spoken word, from the record buyer who asks for a copy of the Queen single "Bohemian Rap City" to the schoolchild who is convinced that the Pledge of Allegiance begins "I led the pigeons to the flag." They tend to be about primal concerns: food, sex, animals. Any misheard lyric is an impromptu audio Rorschach test. It can be alarming to discover that significant parts of our brains want pop songs to cover the lyrical topics of cheese, walruses, and clowns. Songwriters take note: There is a large, untapped market for songs about food.

A good mondegreen lasts for years, and redefines how we hear the song. I had classmates who teased me about my butter dreams well into junior high school. Even when corrected, many people rightly decide that they prefer their version of the song to the one that's actually considered "correct"—and who would deny that "She wore raspberries and grapes" has more poetry in it than the relatively mundane "She wore a raspberry beret"? This book collects some of the best mangled lyrics from dozens of people across the country (including your error-prone author).

Some types of misheard lyrics aren't included in this book. I've excluded instances of people being convinced that a singer was deliberately mouthing nonsense syllables when that singer was doing it accidentally. It delights me to be told when somebody is *convinced* that John Fogerty was singing "Well I'm flan trappa lan" in Creedence Clearwater Revival's "Travelin' Band," rather than the more commonly accepted version of "Well I'm flyin' 'cross the land." But I have decided to leave these examples of gibberish as private testaments to our ability for self-deception.

I have also excluded lyrics that were *deliberately* misheard, no matter how wonderful. My friend Rob Sheffield claims to have believed that Bon Jovi's "Your love is like bad medicine/Bad medicine is what I need" was really of a more literary bent: "Thoreau is like Ralph Emerson/Ralph Emerson is what I read." Delightful as this version is, I don't believe him. However, you, dear reader, may rest assured that all mondegreens in this volume come from authentic mishearings. In some cases, the listener was *very* confused. But do not be too quick to judge their errors. To put myself in a more charitable frame of mind, I need only recall my most embarrassing monde-green moment: singing along at the top of my lungs to a Go-Gos single at a party, convinced that the chorus was not "Our lips are sealed," but "Alex the Seal."

Here's how the mondegreens are organized:

## Wrong lyric

---

**Artist**
**Song title**

---

*Right lyric*

# Clown Control to Mao Tse-Tung

---

**David Bowie**
**"Space Oddity"**

---

*Ground control to Major Tom*

'Scuse me while I kiss this guy

---

**The Jimi Hendrix Experience**
**"Purple Haze"**

---

*'Scuse me while I kiss the sky*

I want to rock 'n' roll all night, and part of every day

---

**Kiss**
**"Rock and Roll All Nite"**

---

*I want to rock 'n' roll all night, and party every day*

It's my parabola

**Bobby Brown**
**"My Prerogative"**

*It's my prerogative*

For he's a delicate fellow

---

**Traditional**
**"For He's a Jolly Good Fellow"**

---

*For he's a jolly good fellow*

Will you still need me, will you still feed me, when
I'm six feet four?

---

**The Beatles**
**"When I'm Sixty-Four"**

---

*. . . when I'm sixty-four?*

- Sore hand in the door
- Soy on my candy corn
- Soul from head to toe
- Boys call me Albert Gore

**Beck**

**"Loser"**

*Soy un perdedor*

You need Kool-Aid, baby I'm not foolin'

---

**Led Zeppelin**
**"Whole Lotta Love"**

---

*You need coolin', baby I'm not foolin'*

It's a hard egg

---

**Bonnie Tyler**
**"It's a Heartache"**

---

*It's a heartache*

I got shoes, they're made of plywood

---

**John Travolta and Olivia Newton-John**
**"You're the One That I Want"**

---

*I got chills, they're multiplying*

Sweet dreams are made of cheese

---

**Eurythmics**
**"Sweet Dreams (Are Made of This)"**

---

*Sweet dreams are made of this*

I do know Mike Ditka

---

**Sinéad O'Connor**
**"Mandinka"**

---

*I do know Mandinka*

All the boys think she's a spaz

---

**Kim Carnes**
**"Bette Davis Eyes"**

---

*All the boys think she's a spy*

# Wake up, I might sit on you

**George Harrison**
**"Got My Mind Set on You"**

*I've got my mind set on you*

We are the Mormons

---

**Asia**
**"Heat of the Moment"**

---

*The heat of the moment*

Sherry don't like it/Rock the catbox

---

**The Clash**
**"Rock the Casbah"**

---

*The Sharif don't like it/Rock the casbah*

Slow-motion Walter, fire-engine guy

---

**Deep Purple**
**"Smoke on the Water"**

---

*Smoke on the water/Fire in the sky*

I have to turn my head and drink from
the garden hose

---

**The Rolling Stones**
**"Paint it Black"**

---

*I have to turn my head until my darkness goes*

Little virus

---

**The Oak Ridge Boys**
**"Elvira"**

---

*Elvira*

The girl with colitis goes by

---

**The Beatles**
**"Lucy in the Sky with Diamonds"**

---

*The girl with kaleidoscope eyes*

# Mice aroma

**The Knack
"My Sharona"**

*My Sharona*

INFESTATION
BY CALVIN KLEIN

White pumps are gauche

---

**The Tubes**
**"White Punks on Dope"**

---

*White punks on dope*


Burn her dead

---

**The Four Tops**
**"Bernadette"**

---

*Bernadette*

That big pineapple cart

---

**The Police**
**"Don't Stand So Close to Me"**

---

*That book by Nabokov*

Singing our faith to the Hustle

---

**The Bee Gees**
**"Nights on Broadway"**

---

*Singing those straight-to-the-heart songs*

Mystery G-men

---

**The Pretenders**
**"Mystery Achievement"**

---

*Mystery achievement*

# Shine on, you crazy blind man

## Pink Floyd
### "Shine on You Crazy Diamond"

*Shine on you crazy diamond*

Take a load of fanny/Take a load for free

---

**The Band**
**"The Weight"**

---

*Take a load off Annie /Take a load for free*

Excellence will happen

---

**Elvis Costello**
**"Accidents Will Happen"**

---

*Accidents will happen*

We will cook Maury Povich

---

**Bob Marley and the Wailers**
**"No Woman No Cry"**

---

*We would cook cornmeal porridge*

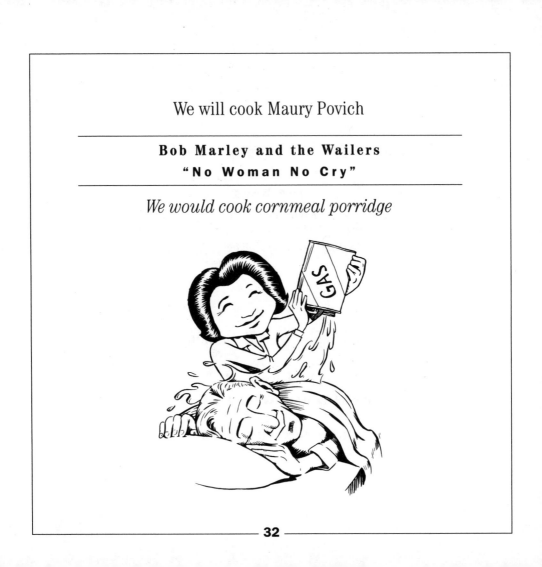

Tryin' to grow

---

**The Doobie Brothers**
**"China Grove"**

---

*China grove*

The problem is you, Rob Lowe

---

**The Sex Pistols**
**"Problems"**

---

*The problem is you . . . problems*

And there's a wino down the road/I should have stolen Oreos

---

**Led Zeppelin**

**"Stairway to Heaven"**

---

*And as we wind on down the road/Our shadows taller than our souls*

Take your pants down and make it happen

---

**Irene Cara**
**"Flashdance . . . What a Feeling"**

---

*Take your passion and make it happen*

Gotta leave it all behind and take a cruise

---

**Queen**
**"Bohemian Rhapsody"**

---

*Gotta leave it all behind and face the truth*

# Baking carrot biscuits

---

## Bachman-Turner Overdrive
## "Takin' Care of Business"

---

*Takin' care of business*

Where you going with the master plan?

---

**Stone Temple Pilots**
**"Plush"**

---

*Where you going with the mask I found?*

Thirty thieves and the thunder chief

---

**AC/DC**
**"Dirty Deeds Done Dirt Cheap"**

---

*Dirty deeds and they're done dirt cheap*

- I am a rock, I am an onion
- I am a rock, I am in Thailand

---

**Simon and Garfunkel**

**"I Am a Rock"**

---

*I am a rock, I am an island*

Every time you go away,
you take a piece of meat with you

---

**Paul Young**

**"Everytime You Go Away"**

---

*. . . you take a piece of me with you*

Secret Asian man

**Johnny Rivers**
**"Secret Agent Man"**

*Secret agent man*

They sell weed and it's wonderful

---

**Elton John**
**"Bennie and the Jets"**

---

*They're so weird and wonderful*


We are punk gods

---

**Nirvana**
**"Smells Like Teen Spirit"**

---

*Load up on guns*

I'm a pool-hall ace

---

**The Police**
**"Every Breath You Take"**

---

*How my poor heart aches*

Hey hey babe, when you walk that way/Got a hunting trip, can't keep away

---

**Led Zeppelin**
**"Black Dog"**

---

*. . . watch honey drip, can't keep away*

Like a drifter I was born to wear cologne

---

**Whitesnake**
**"Here I Go Again"**

---

*Like a drifter I was born to walk alone*

I'm mad about food, you're mad about cheesecake

---

**Belinda Carlisle**
**"Mad About You"**

---

*I'm mad about you, you're mad about me, babe*

Can I believe the magic of your size?

---

**Carole King**
**"Will You Love Me Tomorrow?"**

---

*Can I believe the magic of your sighs?*

• Pinochet
• Hippy shake

---

**The Breeders**
**"Cannonball"**

---

*In the shade*

One man watched on MTV/One man turned
into a fish

---

**U2**

**"Pride (In the Name of Love)"**

---

*One man washed on an empty beach/One man*
*betrayed with a kiss*

Only the lonely get laid

---

**The Motels**
**"Only the Lonely"**

---

*Only the lonely can play*


Cinnamon gum

---

**Steve Perry**
**"Oh Sherrie"**

---

*Should have been gone*

I'm with liverwurst sandwiches

**Bruce Springsteen**
**"Streets of Fire"**

*I live now, only with strangers*

She's got a chicken to ride

**The Beatles**
**"Ticket to Ride"**

*She's got a ticket to ride*

I had a dream, there were clowns in my coffee,
clowns in my coffee

**Carly Simon**

**"You're So Vain"**

*. . . clouds in my coffee*

- It is the wrong umbrella
- It is the arroz con pollo

---

### The Clash
### "Wrong 'Em Boyo"

---

*It is the wrong 'em boyo*

We are ancient Sophocles

---

**R.E.M.**
**"Orange Crush"**

---

*We are agents of the free*

Stop in my neighborhood/Before you break my head

---

**The Supremes**
**"Stop! In the Name of Love"**

---

*Stop! In the name of love/Before you break my heart*

Weenie skin, you and me

---

**R.E.M.**
**"Cuyahoga"**

---

*We knee-skinned, you and me*

- Tell me a jawbreaker
- Only in Jamaica
- Calmly celebrate her

---

**R.E.M.**
**"The Sidewinder Sleeps Tonite"**

---

*Call me when you try to wake her*

Shit! I could lose ya

---

**The Pixies**
**"Debaser"**

---

*Un chien Andalusia*

Still I'm fly-fishing

---

**k.d. lang**
**"Still Thrives This Love"**

---

*Still somehow thrives this love*

Your gum sticks to my hair

---

**Def Leppard**
**"Photograph"**

---

*You've gone straight to my head*

There's a war outside and in my bed

**Neil Young**
**"Rockin' in the Free World"**

*There's a warning sign on the road ahead*

It's funny in Paris

---

**Randy Newman**
**"It's Money That Matters"**

---

*It's money that matters*


I believe in milk and cows

---

**Hot Chocolate**
**"You Sexy Thing"**

---

*I believe in miracles*

• She's so funky, yeah
• She's so popular
• She's so avuncular
• She's so punctual
• She's so fuck-me-now

---

**Peter Gabriel**

**"Games Without Frontiers"**

---

*Jeux sans frontières*

I wanna eat Twinkies with you

---

**Silk**
**"Freak Me"**

---

*I wanna get freaky with you*

- Hair jealousy
- Hey Jodeci

**The Gin Blossoms**
**"Hey Jealousy"**

*Hey jealousy*

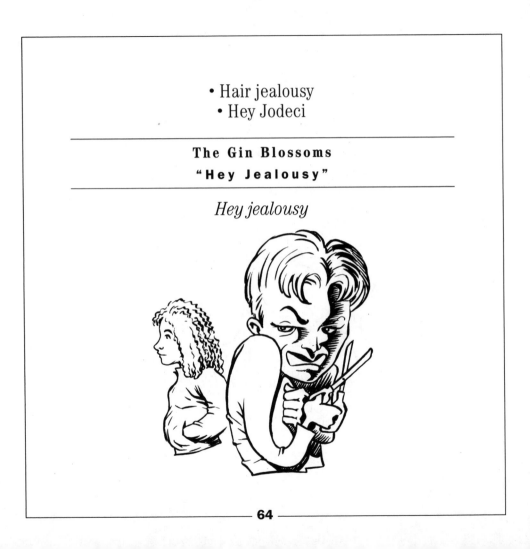

Whoa! Nipsey Russell

---

**The B-52's**
**"Roam"**

---

*Roam, if you want to*


These are the good times/Are you straight or bi?

---

**Chic**
**"Good Times"**

---

*These are the good times/Our new state of mind*

The question to everyone's answer
is usually aspirin with gin

---

**The Steve Miller Band**
**"Jungle Love"**

---

*. . . is usually asked from within*

Life could be ecstasy/Just you and me and Leslie, groovin'

---

**The Rascals**
**"Groovin'"**

---

*Just you and me endlessly groovin'*


Now I'm gonna give you up, now I'm gonna say goodbye

---

**Rick Astley**
**"Never Gonna Give You Up"**

---

*Never gonna give you up, never gonna say goodbye*

- Alex the Seal
- Olives have feelings

---

**The Go-Go's**
**"Our Lips Are Sealed"**

---

*Our lips are sealed*

I want to be just as close as the holy clothespins

---

**Bon Jovi**
**"Bed of Roses"**

---

*I want to be just as close as the Holy Ghost is*

Right on the pea stain

---

**Cat Stevens**
**"Peace Train"**

---

*Ride on the peace train*

Oh give me a home where the buffalo roam, and the deer and the cantaloupe play

**Traditional**
**"Home on the Range"**

*. . . the deer and the antelope play*

I heard aroma

---

**Bananarama**
**"I Heard a Rumour"**

---

*I heard a rumour*

And when he died/All he left us was a lawn

---

**The Temptations**
**"Papa Was a Rollin' Stone"**

---

*. . . all he left us was alone*

- She wore raspberries and grapes
- She wore rags, very good rags

---

**Prince and the Revolution**
**"Raspberry Beret"**

---

*She wore a raspberry beret*

I've got a Swedish hangover

---

**Diana Ross**
**"Love Hangover"**

---

*I've got the sweetest hangover*

Travesty

---

**Sniff 'n' the Tears**
**"Driver's Seat"**

---

*Driver's seat*

She's the kind of girl who makes a musical fail

---

**The Beatles**
**"Polythene Pam"**

---

*She's the kind of girl who makes* The News of the World

Salivate on a padlocked door

---

**The Rolling Stones**
**"Bitch"**

---

*Salivate like Pavlov's dog*

Mama say mama saw my moccasin

---

**Michael Jackson**
**"Wanna Be Startin' Somethin'"**

---

*Ma ma se ma ma sa ma ma coo sa*


Living in the Bronx, it's a put-on

---

**The Who**
**"Eminence Front"**

---

*Eminence front, it's a put-on*

I wanna be a wombat, I wanna be anemic

**Soul II Soul**
**"Back to Life"**

*However do you want me, however do you need me*

I got seven women on my mind/Four of them want to
hold me, two of them want to scold me

---

**The Eagles**
**"Take It Easy"**

---

*. . . four that wanna own me, two that wanna*
*stone me*

They call her a tramp/I can't walk out

---

**Elvis Presley**
**"Suspicious Minds"**

---

*We're caught in a trap/I can't walk out*

Salami, salami

---

**The Police**
**"So Lonely"**

---

*So lonely, so lonely*

Last night I dreamt of some bagels

---

**Madonna**
**"La Isla Bonita"**

---

*Last night I dreamt of San Pedro*

And you believe in that chunky stew

*And you believe all that junk is true*

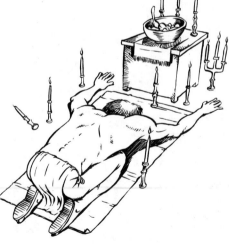

# Calling Underdog

## The Doors
## "The Soft Parade"

*Calling on the dogs*

I'm a loser baby, so why don't you call me?

**Beck**
**"Loser"**

*I'm a loser baby, so why don't you kill me?*

Hey, wait, I've got a naked plate

**Nirvana**
**"Heart-Shaped Box"**

*. . . I've got a new complaint*

There's a feeling I get when I look at my waist

---

**Led Zeppelin**
**"Stairway to Heaven"**

---

*There's a feeling I get when I look to the west*

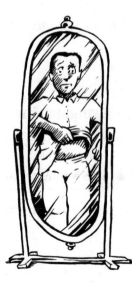

Efficient finger-pies

---

**The Beatles**
**"Penny Lane"**

---

*Fish and finger-pies*

Who's gonna shave me?

---

**Midnight Oil**
**"Blue Sky Mining"**

---

*Who's gonna save me?*

# One-ton tomato

## Traditional
## "Guantanamera"

*Guantanamera*

Sixteen Colombian children

---

**The Smiths**
**"Half a Person"**

---

*Sixteen, clumsy, and shy*

Find myself a great historic place

---

**Counting Crows**
**"Mr. Jones"**

---

*Buy myself a gray guitar and play*

I'll eat you like a chocolate

---

**Madonna**
**"Erotica"**

---

*I'll hit you like a truck*


Keep it common-law

---

**KC and the Sunshine Band**
**"Keep it Comin' Love"**

---

*Keep it comin', love*

Don't eat the reefer

---

**Blue Oyster Cult**
**"(Don't Fear) The Reaper"**

---

*Don't fear the reaper*

Give me one last chance/We'll slide down
the circus of pigs

---

**U2**
**"Even Better Than the Real Thing"**

---

*. . . we'll slide down the surface of things*

# There's a bathroom on the right

## Creedence Clearwater Revival
### "Bad Moon Rising"

*There's a bad moon on the rise*

Strong as Naugahyde

---

**Blondie**
**"Heart of Glass"**

---

*Love is far behind*

My anus will fix it, you're addicted to love

---

**Robert Palmer**
**"Addicted to Love"**

---

*Might as well face it, you're addicted to love*

Stretch marks for dollars

---

**Tina Turner**
**"Private Dancer"**

---

*Deutschmarks for dollars*

I'll tell a lawyer

---

**Culture Club**
**"I'll Tumble 4 Ya"**

---

*I'll tumble for ya*

- Beijing ain't high enough
- Maybe an iron lung

---

**Steve Winwood**

**"Higher Love"**

---

*Bring me a higher love*

Lettuce now kiss the cornbread

**The Velvet Underground**
**"Some Kinda Love"**

*Let us now kiss the culprit*

Ain't no woman like the one-eyed Gott

---

**The Four Tops**
**"Ain't No Woman"**

---

*Ain't no woman like the one I've got*


Where was the thunder?

---

**Warren Zevon**
**"Werewolves of London"**

---

*Werewolves of London*

- Four-legged woman
- Bald-headed woman

---

**The Bee Gees**

**"More than a Woman"**

---

*More than a woman*

I just can't get it up

---

**Depeche Mode**
**"Just Can't Get Enough"**

---

*I just can't get enough*

With a purple operator and fifty-cent hair

---

**Led Zeppelin**
**"Living Loving Maid**
**(She's Just a Woman)"**

---

*With a purple umbrella and a fifty-cent hat*

Little bitty cows for you and me

---

**John Cougar Mellencamp**
**"Pink Houses"**

---

*Little pink houses for you and me*

But I get no offers/Just a come-on from the horse on Seventh Avenue

---

**Simon and Garfunkel**
**"The Boxer"**

---

*. . . the whores on Seventh Avenue*

- Remember what the doorknob said
- Remember what the dogma said

---

**Jefferson Airplane**

**"White Rabbit"**

---

*Remember what the dormouse said*

I'm not the cat I used to be/I've got a can of thirty-three babies

---

**The Pretenders**

**"Middle of the Road"**

---

*I've got a kid, I'm thirty-three, baby*

Well I dig a little dog about an hour ago

**The Doors**

**"L.A. Woman"**

*Well I just got into town about an hour ago*

And you were waiting there/Swimming
through a pile of cheese

**Berlin**

**"The Metro"**

*. . . swimming through apologies*

Looks like tomatoes

---

**Barry Manilow**
**"Looks Like We Made It"**

---

*Looks like we made it*


Jethro! What a brother knows

---

**Public Enemy**
**"Bring the Noise"**

---

*Death row!*

We can try/What is that?/New York has
the baseball games

---

**The Bee Gees**
**"Stayin' Alive"**

---

*We can try to understand/* The New York Times's
*effect on man*


My candelabra

---

**Billy Squier**
**"My Kind of Lover"**

---

*My kind of lover*

They hit you with a wrecking ball

---

**Tears for Fears**
**"Shout"**

---

*They took you for a working boy*

- It's such a feeling that, my love, I get hives
- It's such a feeling that, my love, I get high

---

**The Beatles**

**"I Want to Hold Your Hand"**

---

*. . . I can't hide*

Sweet, sweet vasectomy

---

**Sting**
**"If You Love Somebody Set Them Free"**

---

*Free, free, set them free*

Every time I hear your name/I always
catch my breasts

---

**John Waite**
**"Missing You"**

---

*I always catch my breath*

The Dukes of Hazzard are in the classroom

---

**Pink Floyd**
**"Another Brick in the Wall (Part 2)"**

---

*No dark sarcasm in the classroom*

Strut now, cut it out, no talking on Thanksgiving

---

**Sheena Easton**
**"Strut"**

---

*Strut, pout, cut it out,*
*no taking and no giving*

Love will get you like a case of Ex-Lax

---

**Gang of Four**
**"Anthrax"**

---

*Love will get you like a case of anthrax*

She sees the hat rack, is she going to touch it?

**Genesis**
**"Invisible Touch"**

*She seems to have that invisible touch, yeah*

# Reagan rots in the hot sun

## The Clash
## "I Fought the Law"

*Breaking rocks in the hot sun*

You picked a fine time to leave me, Lucille/
With four hundred children

---

**Kenny Rogers**
**"Lucille"**

---

*. . . with four hungry children*

Lice! Lice! Lice! Yeah!

---

**Thompson Twins**
**"Lies"**

---

*Lies! Lies! Lies! Yeah!*

If I had a rocking lawn chair

---

**Bruce Cockburn**
**"If I Had a Rocket Launcher"**

---

*If I had a rocket launcher*

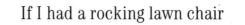

- Jeremy smoked grass today
- Jeremy broke glass today
- Sara Lee Smoked Ham

---

**Pearl Jam**
**"Jeremy"**

---

*Jeremy spoke in class today*

Chug-a-lug, strawberry man

**Steve Miller Band**
**"Jungle Love"**

*Jungle love is drivin' me mad*

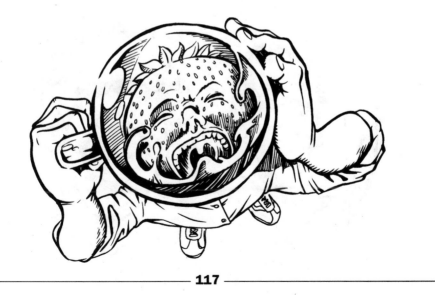

She's like Fred Gwynne, in my dreams

**Patrick Swayze**
**"She's Like the Wind"**

*She's like the wind*

Medieval woman

**Electric Light Orchestra**
**"Evil Woman"**

*Evil woman*

Just brush my teeth before you leave me, baby

**Juice Newton**
**"Angel of the Morning"**

*Just touch my cheek before you leave me, baby*

The birds are all filled up with juice

---

**Crowded House**
**"Locked Out"**

---

*The birds are offering up their tunes*

Sunday monkey won't play piano song,
play piano song

**The Beatles**
**"Michelle"**

*Sont des mots qui vont très bien ensemble/*
*Très bien ensemble*

Apartheid lover

---

**Stevie Wonder**
**"Part-Time Lover"**

---

*A part-time lover*


Throws her panties off in the hall

---

**L 7**
**"Fast and Frightening"**

---

*Sets M-80s off in the hall*

# The smell of my check

### David Bowie
### "Suffragette City"

*This mellow-thighed chick*

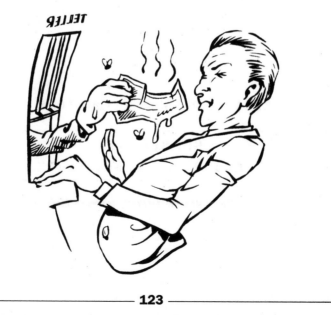

Don't tell me when I want a beer

**Nirvana**
**"Lounge Act"**

*Don't tell me what I want to hear*

And you were Michael Caine et al.

**Gin Blossoms**
**"Found Out About You"**

*And you were mine, forget it all*

- She's got electric boobs, her mom has two
  - She's got a lot of booze, Samoan Sue

**Elton John**
**"Bennie and the Jets"**

*She's got electric boots, a mohair suit*

Forty-five versions of a pelican

---

**Pearl Jam**
**"Glorified G"**

---

*Glorified version of a pellet gun*

# Choke the walrus

**Pearl Jam**
**"Go"**

*Don't go on me*

Balled all of the women, came and wept,
barefoot surfers too

---

**The Jimi Hendrix Experience**
**"All Along the Watchtower"**

---

*While all of the women came and went,
barefoot servants, too*

When Jupiter collides with Mars

---

**The 5th Dimension**
**"Aquarius"**

---

*When Jupiter aligns with Mars*

Hush hush, deeper downtown, it's so scary

---

**'Til Tuesday**
**"Voices Carry"**

---

*Hush hush, keep it down now, voices carry*


We'll keep on farting until the end

---

**Queen**
**"We Are the Champions"**

---

*We'll keep on fighting until the end*

# Who got a smoking caterpillar?

**Jefferson Airplane**
**"White Rabbit"**

*A hookah-smoking caterpillar*

You dropped a dog on me

---

**The Gap Band**
**"You Dropped a Bomb on Me"**

---

*You dropped a bomb on me*

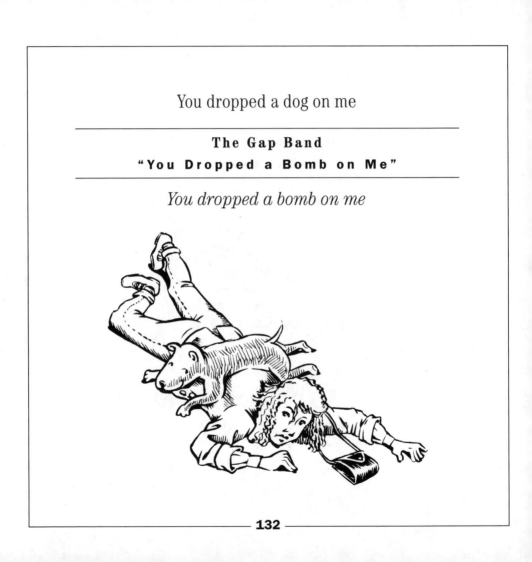

Every day might turn fuchsia rose

---

**New Order**
**"Bizarre Love Triangle"**

---

*Every day my confusion grows*



They sent you a tie clasp

---

**Elvis Presley**
**"Hound Dog"**

---

*They said you was high-class*

Get your rock salt, get your rock salt baby

---

**Primal Scream**
**"Rocks"**

---

*Get your rocks off, get your rocks off baby*


The way she brushed her hair and farted

---

**Paul Simon**
**"Graceland"**

---

*The way she brushed her hair from her forehead*

Dogs play bass for human beings

---

**Machines of Loving Grace**
**"Butterfly Wings"**

---

*Don't place faith in human beings*

I sat in the sherbet

**Bob Marley and the Wailers**
**"I Shot the Sheriff"**

*I shot the sheriff*

Kick her in the crotch

---

**Michael Jackson**
**"Keep It In the Closet"**

---

*Keep it in the closet*

• I'm not talking about religion
• I'm not talking about the linen

---

**England Dan & John Ford Coley**
**"I'd Really Love to See You Tonight"**

---

*I'm not talking about moving in*

Dumber babe

---

**Pavement**
**"Summer Babe"**

---

*Summer babe*


Think we'll keep on turning?

---

**Ike and Tina Turner**
**"Proud Mary"**

---

*Big wheel keep on turning*

I'm running down a drain

---

**Tom Petty**
**"Runnin' Down a Dream"**

---

*I'm running down a dream*

If we can solve any problem/Why do we lose
so many teeth?

---

**Paul Young**
**"Everytime You Go Away"**

---

*Why do we lose so many tears?*

My anus is the centerhole

---

**J. Geils Band**
**"Centerfold"**

---

*My angel is the centerfold*

You don't need a pinhead just to hang around

---

**Creedence Clearwater Revival**
**"Down on the Corner"**

---

*You don't need a penny just to hang around*

# Ninety-five fingers

**Pearl Jam**
**"Rearviewmirror"**

*United by fear*

I'll proceed from shame

**Nirvana**
**"All Apologies"**

*Aqua seafoam shame*


And the papers want to know who shot you where

**David Bowie**
**"Space Oddity"**

*And the papers want to know whose shirts you wear*

I'd like to keep my cheese dry today

---

**Blind Melon**
**"No Rain"**

---

*I'd like to keep my cheeks dry today*

Don't chew on me, baby

**The Human League
"Don't You Want Me"**

*Don't you want me, baby?*

How's about a date?

---

**Billy Idol**
**"Eyes Without a Face"**

---

*Eyes without a face*


Goodbye yellow brick road/With the darkened
sorority house

---

**Elton John**
**"Goodbye Yellow Brick Road"**

---

*. . . where the dogs of society howl*

# Life in the Vaseline

## The Eagles
## "Life in the Fast Lane"

*Life in the fast lane*

# Climb every woman

---

**Chaka Khan**
**"I'm Every Woman"**

---

*I'm every woman*

And doughnuts make my brown eyes blue

---

**Crystal Gayle**
**"Don't It Make My Brown Eyes Blue"**

---

*And don't it make my brown eyes blue*

I been doin' it since I was a young kid and
I come up redneck

**John Cougar Mellencamp**
**"Authority Song"**

*I come up grinnin'*

I'm gonna make you, make you, make you malteds

**The Pretenders**
**"Brass in Pocket"**

*. . . make you notice*

Baby I'm a warm shoe, baby I'm a neat shoe

---

**Bread**
**"Baby I'm-a Want You"**

---

*Baby I'm-a want you, baby I'm-a need you*

She was a state trooper

---

**The Beatles**
**"Day Tripper"**

---

*She was a day tripper*

Everybody's got a hungry horse

**Bruce Springsteen**
**"Hungry Heart"**

*Everybody's got a hungry heart*

# Franciscans in the U.S.A.

**Debbie Harry**
**"French Kissin' in the U.S.A."**

*French kissin' in the U.S.A.*

I am not into health food/I add hemp to champagne

---

**Rupert Holmes**
**"Escape (The Piña Colada Song)"**

---

*. . . I am into champagne*

Jacques the monkey

**Peter Gabriel**
**"Shock the Monkey"**

*Shock the monkey*

- Forty-seven
- Bony Sartre

---

**Steely Dan**
**"Bodhisattva"**

---

*Bodhisattva*


No fuchsia, no fuchsia, no fuchsia for you

---

**The Sex Pistols**
**"God Save the Queen"**

---

*No future, no future, no future for you*

- I'm blotto and bravado/I'm a scarecrow and a Beatle
- I'm Nirvana, I'm Nirvana/You're a shaker, have a beer

---

### Nirvana
### "Smells Like Teen Spirit"

---

*A mulatto, an albino/A mosquito, my libido*

But the chair is not my size

**Michael Jackson**
**"Billie Jean"**

*But the kid is not my son*

The ants are my friends/They're blowin' in the wind

**Bob Dylan**
**"Blowin' in the Wind"**

*The answer, my friends, is blowin' in the wind*

It's no fun, living in a neon area

*It's no fun, being an illegal alien*

• She ripped up her douche in the middle of the night
• Wrapped up like a douche/Another boner in the night

---

**Manfred Mann's Earth Band**
**"Blinded by the Light"**

---

*Revved up like a deuce/Another runner in the night*

With a box of Thin Mints, I don't wanna pay the rent

---

**Jane's Addiction**
**"Been Caught Stealing"**

---

*When I want something, man, I don't want*
*to pay for it*

You were counting on your ovaries

---

**Billy Joel**
**"Only the Good Die Young"**

---

*You were counting on your rosaries*

Grapefruit through the night

---

**The National Anthem**

---

*Gave proof through the night*

# I built this goddamn forest

**Lenny Kravitz**
**"I Build This Garden for Us"**

*I build this garden for us*

Olive, my love

**Led Zeppelin**
**"All My Love"**

*All of my love*

Lady Elaine, lay across my big brass bed

---

**Bob Dylan**
**"Lay Lady Lay"**

---

*Lay lady lay, lay across my big brass bed*

I like smokin' ice cream

---

**Steppenwolf**
**"Born to Be Wild"**

---

*I like smoke and lightning*

Who needs to drink when your teeth just glow?

**Tom Tom Club**
**"Genius of Love"**

*Who needs to think when your feet just go?*

I wanna be a dork

---

**The Stone Roses**
**"I Wanna Be Adored"**

---

*I wanna be adored*

My heels are alive with the sound of music

---

**The Sound of Music Original Cast**
**"The Sound of Music"**

---

*The hills are alive with the sound of music*

We're giving love/To the family dog

---

**Sister Sledge**
**"We Are Family"**

---

*We're giving love/In a family dose*

- Ego Jan and the rhino
- Pink hotel in Carolina
- Bingo Jed and Lionel
- We don't chat at a lighthouse

---

**Steve Miller Band**

**"Jet Airliner"**

---

*Big ol' jet airliner*

# Tuna hot-dog

## Van McCoy
## "The Hustle"

*Do the hustle*

EDITOR'S NOTE: NO DOLPHINS WERE INJURED IN THE DRAWING OF THIS HOT DOG

There's a problem over Zion, burning buildings

---

**R.E.M.**
**"Fall on Me"**

---

*There's the problem: feathers, iron,*
*bargain buildings*

Time I had some Tylenol

---

**R.E.M.**
**"It' the End of the World as We Know It**
**(and I Feel Fine)"**

---

*Time I had some time alone*

# Shamu in mysterious ways

## U2
### "Mysterious Ways"

*She moves in mysterious ways*

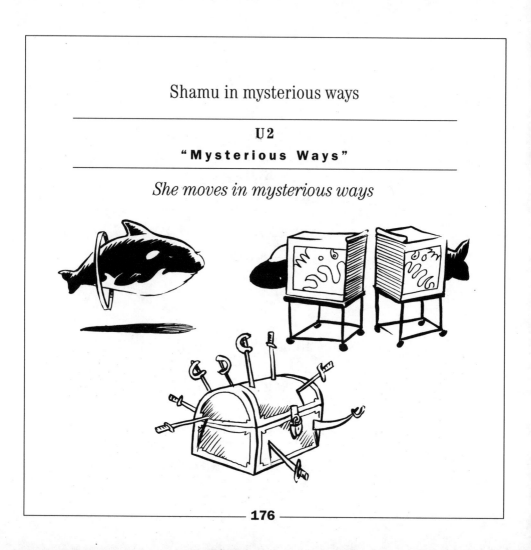

I like it kinky

**Simple Minds**
**"Alive & Kicking"**

*Alive and kicking*

Lay down the salad

**Eric Clapton**
**"Lay Down Sally"**

*Lay down, Sally*

The gravy stands alone

**Stone Temple Pilots**
**"Plush"**

*Where she stands alone*

I look at you and the patient dies

**P.M. Dawn**
**"Looking Through Patient Eyes"**

*I look at you with patient eyes*

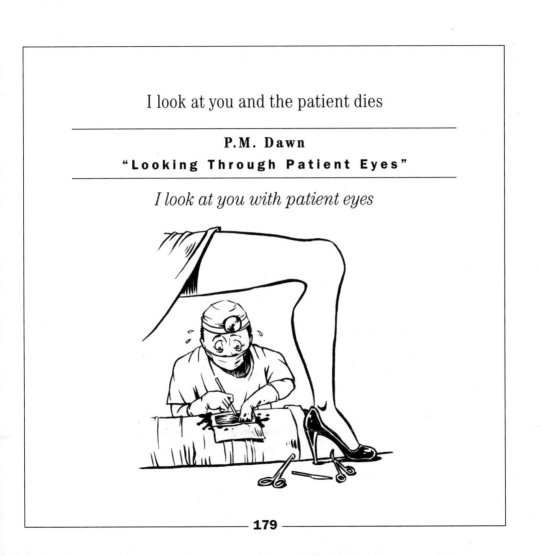

There are spirits eating my Cheerios

---

**The Police**
**"Spirits in the Material World"**

---

*We are spirits in the material world*

It's Saturday night/Have you seen my legs?

---

**Elton John**
**"Saturday Night's Alright for Fighting"**

---

*It's gettin' late/Have yer seen my mates?*

A rooster or maybe even an idiot cheese

---

**Rose Royce**
**"Car Wash"**

---

*A movie star or maybe even an Indian chief*

I'll never leave your pizza burnin'

---

**The Rolling Stones**
**"Beast of Burden"**

---

*I'll never be your beast of burden*

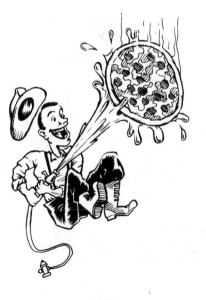

Where we're goin', the pine cones run in and make
tonight a wonderful thing

---

**Steely Dan**

**"Hey Nineteen"**

---

*The Cuervo Gold, the fine Colombian, make tonight
a wonderful thing*

In the chocolate madness

**Jethro Tull**
**"Locomotive Breath"**

*In the shuffling madness*

# Acknowledgments

Although more of this book comes from my own unreliable ears than I would like to admit, the vast majority comes from others who generously shared their own mondegreens or gleefully passed on the mistakes of friends. In a few cases, musicians gleefully repeated their fans' errors. I am eternally grateful to: Matt Aibel, Lily J. Anderson, Leigh Angel, Val Azari, Julia Baker, Amy Barefoot, Larry Berger, Nils Bernstein, Kat Bjelland, Daniel Blackman, Brian Blank, Ned Boynton, Susan Campbell, Phil Catalfo, Skye Michele Chasnov, Keith Chilcutt, Jeff Christian, Chris Clark, Laura Collings, Kim Corbett, Steve Crystal, Marnie Davis, Jennifer Dellapina, Dennis Dennehy, Bob d'Entremont, Erika M. Delph, Guy Doherty, Molly Dunne, Regina Joskow Dunton, Tim Earp, Lisa A. Ellis, Ilsa Enomoto, Joanne P. Evans, David Ferrini, Jennifer Finch, Erik Flannigan, Sue Fleming-Holland, Stacy Fraser, Ted Friedman, George Gallucci, Sharon Ganelli, Suzi Gardner, Lisa Jo Gilliam, Bradley Glenn, Joe Greene, Vince Grindstaff, Angela Gunn, Dawn Hannaham, James Hannaham,

Chris Harris, Lynn Harris, Jonathan Hayes, Mark Heggen, Sarah Hotze, Elizabeth Hurchalla, Christie Ingenito, Chris M. Junior, Jonathan Kulick, Suzanna Laine, Cindi Leive, Kate Lewis, Lisa Lippman, Julia Litton, Sheryl Lynch, Carol E. Mariconela, Mike Matey, Kevin McPherson, Tim Miske, John Neilson, Jeff Neuman, Emily Nussbaum, Martha Otis, Kimberly Passey, Gy H. Art Pe, Stacy Jordan Pershall, Richard Polito, Corey S. Powell, Erica Prodouz, Jeanie Pyun, Sam Ragsdale, Anne Rieman, Edvard Rutmanis, C. A. Schneck, Margaret Segall, H. Hillary Seitz, Rob Sheffield, Conrad M. Sienkiewicz, Mike Silverman, Leslie Singer, Kent Sponagle, Jenny Stein, Tima Surmelioglu, David Sweet, Rick Telander, Mim Udovitch, Scott Underwood, Joe Utsler, Maggie Vaisman, Melissa Welch, Kimberly Wheatley, Louisa Winer, Luke Wood, Clay Matthew Wright, Christi J. York, Margaret Young, and Julie Zwillick.

If you have misheard lyrics of your own, I would love to include them in a sequel to this book. Please send them to: Gavin Edwards, P.O. Box 023291, Brooklyn, NY 11202-3291. Hurry—I can only acknowledge the first person to send me each mondegreen.

Special thanks to Jon Carroll, who generously shared his own misheard lyrics and filled the gaps in my mondegreen history, and Frank Kogan, distinguished mondegreen scholar, who gave me access to his treasure trove.

This book began life as a series of articles in *Details* magazine. Thanks to Steve Bodow, who sparked that series, and to everybody at *Details* and Condé Nast who helped make this volume a reality, especially James Truman, John Leland, Lisa Murray, Karen Rinaldi, David Keeps, Tommy Dunne, Lance Kaplan, Cindy Hoag, George Pelletier, Eric Thurnauer, Chris Moore, Mike Dolan, and Diana Edkins.

I am deeply indebted to three very talented men: Gordon Kato, agent extraordinaire; Dave Dunton, who edited this book with flair and wit; and Chris Kalb, whose drawings brought it to life. This book might have happened without them, but it would be vastly poorer for their absence.

And I extend my warmest thanks to every singer who ever stinted on his or her enunciation. Without them, this book would not exist.